HEALING
WITH THE
POWER
OF YOUR
MIND

HEALING
WITH THE
POWER
OF YOUR
MIND

CHANTHA PAK

Author Chantha Pak
ChanthaPak@outlook.com
www.ChanthaPak.com

Bulk order requests for organizations or book clubs can also be sent to the email address above.

The author of this book does not dispense medical advice or prescribe the use of any technique as a form of treatment for physical, emotional, or medical problems without the advice of a physician, either directly or indirectly. The intent of the author is only to offer information of a general nature to help you in your quest for spiritual and physical well-being. In the event you use any of the information in this book for yourself, the author and publisher assume no responsibility for your actions.

Cover design by Damien Mayfield, DamienMayfield.com
Editing and interior design by Tanya Brockett, HallagenInk.com

Printed in the United States of America

CONTENTS

FOREWORD

Dr. Joe Vitale

Healing is what this world needs right now.

Not only have we been through a global pandemic that impacted the physical health of millions, but the lives and mental health of many have been turned upside down and are in need of healing too.

This book is the antidote. This book shows you how YOU can be the cure for all that ails you.

Like me, Chantha has studied the masters of metaphysics and new thought for years, and has applied her understanding of the Universal Laws to her own life. Her amazing journey from death's door to vibrance and vitality will amaze you. But even more, it will show you how you can get in alignment with what I have called, The Great Something, and make miracles happen in your life.

I get it. It can be a challenge to look at your current reality, what Chantha calls "the manifested condition," and believe that there is something better. But as I have said in my book *The*

Attractor Factor and others, your current reality can change. It is the result of your past thoughts and actions. Now, you can let go of the negativity and shift to something better. Or "shew it away like you shew a fly," as Chantha says.

Like me, Chantha knows that we are all attractors of our experiences. When you awaken to the Universal Laws, you recognize you are no longer a victim of circumstances, but a deliberate creator of your life and results.

To be that deliberate creator, you have to release the fear, negativity, and limiting beliefs that hold you back. In my book, *The Miracle*, I call these counterintentions. If you want to create a healthy body or life, you not only have to identify what you want, and get into the feeling place of having it, but you have to let go of the counterintentions that block your manifestation.

The simple three-steps to healing that Chantha shares in this book will help you turn away from your "manifested conditions," and set you on the path to healing (your body and your life). The more you tap into your intuition and take inspired action, the easier it will become.

The meditations provided for you at the end of the book will help you to get into alignment for receiving your highest good. I like doing affirmations with healing music in the background (like *At Zero* or *Invoking Divinity* music), but as long as you are in action, that is what matters most.

If you are finally ready to let go of pain in your body, illness, or simply negative circumstances infecting your life, read this book. Keep it by your side whenever you need to be reminded that you have the Infinite Intelligence within you that can aid in your healing.

Read, heal, and *Expect Miracles*.

Joe Vitale, D.MSc.
Author, *Zero Limits* and *The Miracle*
Host, "Zero Limits Living" e-TV
www.MrFire.com

INTRODUCTION

An open mind opens the door to true healing.

They called me the walking dead. No one could comprehend how someone with so little blood in their body could still be walking. Doctors had never seen anyone survive that. So, how am I here to talk about it? I opened the door to the power of my mind.

I am so grateful this book has found its way to you.

If you have physical issues, ailments, pains, and illnesses that you want to release from your body, this book will certainly help you to do that. Everything I share in this book has allowed me to heal from what could have been a fatal diagnosis so I could thrive with ease and grace.

You can also use the powerful principles in this book if you are not ill. You can use it as preventative medicine to stay healthy and whole. This book will help you to maintain good health deliberately and consistently generate the positive vibration that leads to health. It will help you to keep your mind and body strong so that no disease will become an issue for you.

I have been a student of the great masters of Universal Laws—like Florence Scovel Shinn and Neville Goddard—for many years. They have allowed me to create miracles in my life, both through healing and in other ways. In this book, I will share with you the principles that I live by every day. I see them manifest in my life and I know how powerful and effective they are. Those I have had the pleasure of sharing this information with have benefited greatly from their new understanding and belief. My daughter is a powerful example of this. She is now so in tune with her Inner Being that she knows how to identify when she is out of alignment. If she is at work and runs into an angry client, she knows she needs to realign by doing the inner work that allows her outer world to reflect it.

That can be true for you as well.

- *If you have suffered from chronic pain and have a hard time believing that you will ever be pain-free, this book is for you.*
- *If you have recently been diagnosed with a terminal or debilitating illness, this book is for you.*
- *If you have a constantly recurring illness year after year, this book is for you.*
- *If you have a family history of disease and fear that you are next, this book is for you.*
- *If you are healthy and want to know how to secure your continued good health going forward, this book is for you.*

Within these pages you will learn that you have the power to shift all negative situations. You will come to understand the Universal Laws that determine your results. You will learn how to use the power of your mind to create new, positive situations in your life. You will discover how your body is an instrument that your mind can control. And you will learn how powerful you truly are, not only in your own health, but in your overall life.

The principles herein will not only apply to your physical health, but to every area of your life. Though my focus is on healing, you can use these same principles to positively impact your relationships, your finances, your career, your business, your community contributions, and your joy in everyday living.

Inside these pages, you will not just find theory and be told to blindly apply it. You will be guided to your understanding of the Universal Laws and how you can practically apply them to your life. I will show you by example how I have used these Laws in my own life and in the lives of others, so you can see how it can work for you.

It is my desire and intention for you to feel a sense of relief when you finish this book. I want you to know that you have the power to create health and healing in your own body and world. I want you to see the evidence of it almost immediately. Once you start putting these principles into action in your own life, you will begin to see your manifested reality shift to match it.

I designed the book to present practical approaches to exercising the power of your mind. You will find tips, steps, actions you can take, and evidence-based examples to help you see what is possible. I will repeat important principles throughout the book deliberately, because I want you to really soak them in. Then, with practice, you will be able to grow in your understanding of these approaches, apply them, and begin to trust and know that you, too, have the power to heal.

Your body is a wellness-producing machine. Help it to fulfill that purpose by exercising the power of your mind to heal. Read the book all the way through and practice what you resonate with as it occurs. Then read it again and focus on the portions of the book you are drawn to most. You will attract the information that you need. Review and practice, and practice some more, until you get this down in your spirit and take to heart all that is shared. Know that you can heal with the power of your mind. Know that you can create a positive life experience for yourself. Test it. Watch the impact. Take joy in your results. And keep your tank filled to the brim with positive energy so that you can continue to attract only goodness, abundance, good health, and wholeness in your life. That is my wish for you.

—Chantha

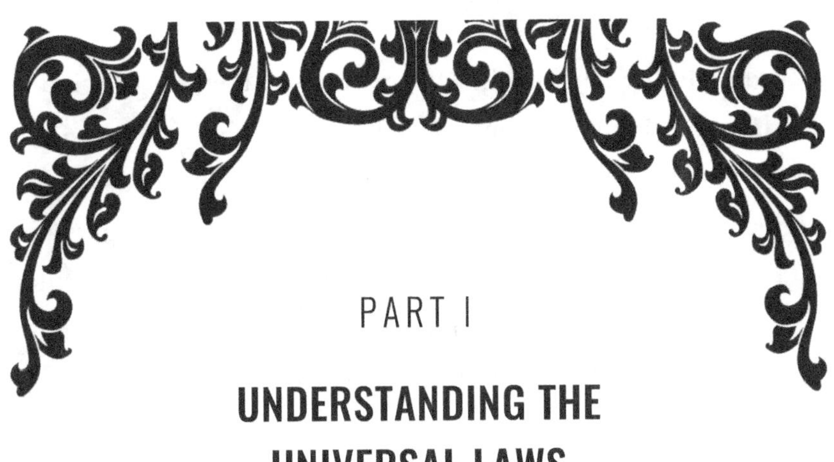

PART I

UNDERSTANDING THE UNIVERSAL LAWS

*"By the powerful law of attraction, that
which is like unto itself is drawn."*

—Abraham-Hicks

We are living in a universe of law and order. What we think goes out into the universal subjective mind, which is Law, and returns to us that which we think upon. Our thought is an intelligence and has power to objectify through the creative medium of the universe and create the things we think about. Science has discovered that when a man thinks, there is a reaction to his thoughts and all his affairs and bodily conditions are affected by his thinking.

Everything you experience in your life, whether health, wealth, happiness, or relationships, is a projection from your state of consciousness, or thoughts, combined with feelings, desires, and beliefs. Nothing can happen by chance or by luck. It comes according to the Laws of the Universe, which are laws of mind—mental law. It is an invisible unseen force.

What we send out, in other words, we create in our own lives. We create what we think about. You can change your thoughts and beliefs, and then the outer experience must change too. The outer experience cannot change until you first change your inner thoughts. The outside mirrors the inside. Outer things can't change until we change.

For example, it is like looking in the mirror and expecting the image to change. It cannot change until you do. You have to change for the reflection to change.

If you are feeling unhappy or if you are worried or feeling resentful or have any negative feelings (resistance), you cannot attract the positive things you want. And if you are feeling happy and uplifted or joyful, you are opening the valve to what you want. The way you feel causes the attraction.

For example, if you want money, feel the feeling of wealth and abundance. What would you feel like if you had it? And if you are wanting to have a healthy body, what would you feel like if you had that healthy body? What activities would you perform if you were well? Imagine the things you would do. Close your eyes for a moment and feel the feeling of doing all those activities that you love to do; imagine those activities in your mind, and feel the joy of doing them in your body. Then open your eyes and release those positive thoughts and feelings to the Universe. Those imagined desires will then become real for you just as you desired and imagined them. As long as you don't doubt it or have resistance, you will not block it.

> *"Imagination is everything. It is the preview of life's coming attraction."*
>
> —Albert Einstein

If you have resistance, your desires cannot come. The desire without resistance makes it manifest, which is pure desire. So you will know you are in alignment with your desire by the way you feel; your emotion is your guidance system. If you are not feeling good, stop and think. Catch any resistance early before the momentum gets too strong. And then you control your point of attraction before it starts to manifest. You come into this world to create what you want with your mind, which is connected with Infinite Intelligence. You have an Inner Being, which some may call God, and what you ask of God, believing you will have it, is given to you. All the great scientists, seers, poets, inventors, and teachers of the past have known this Law.

It Works in the Negative Too

What if what you want is negativity? If somebody is throwing a tantrum, they will keep finding reasons to have a pity party. You can't get what you want if you're in a negative state, but that's assuming that what you want something positive.

If you want to whine and complain, spend enough time doing so and you will create more to whine and complain about. You will even find other people to whine and complain with you! But if all you do is whine and complain about not having a better life, that better life cannot come to you. It's an opposite energy. You cannot attract the thing you want by complaining about the problem. The complaint becomes a perpetual cycle or downward spiral. You will experience the same situation day after day.

And the more you focus your attention on the negative things that keep happening day after day, the more they keep showing up for you. You have to stop the merry-go-round in order to get off without hurting yourself. You have to put your attention on something positive if you want things to change positively, because the Universe picks up your energy and your vibration and sends back to you what you are focusing on with emotion.

What You Think, You Attract

It is important to understand how our thoughts get out into the ether and return back to us. Our lives are created by the way we think, feel, and believe. Things just don't happen at random, though many people think they do. For instance, people watch the news and leave their minds open to all kinds of negativity being reported. They just let what they are listening to and feeling badly about into their minds without realizing, "Oh, this thought goes out to the Universe, and then returns back to me whatever I'm thinking and feeling."

So, things don't just happen. We create them with our thoughts and our feelings and our beliefs. Know that you have the power to control what comes into your life and how to create it.

You now know why things happen the way they happen, so be aware of that.

Realizing there's a Law that works according to your thinking, feeling, and belief, you know how to control what comes into your life. Now when you start to reflect on, "Oh, why did I get this? What was I thinking?" You can retrace those steps. You know that the Universe operates by Law; it doesn't just send you things that you're not in vibrational harmony with. You have to be on that wavelength, on that frequency, to receive it.

You decide what you want to wear, what you want to eat, where you want to go, and with whom to do all those things, but you don't always decide your thoughts. You don't always decide what you want to think about. You just let a negative thought take over. And when you think on it long enough, by the powerful Law of Attraction, that negative thought turns into a negative situation. So choose your thoughts wisely in order to attract only the things you want.

Our world is 99 percent mental, not physical. Get the mental aspect right and the physical things will fall into place.

Understanding how the Universe operates by mental law, you start to shift your thinking and change it. You can't be thinking in the old way, like being worried about getting a disease that someone you know has. You have to have mind control and not live in worry or fear. Now that you understand this Law, guide your mind to focus on something positive or read a good book. That upliftment will change the energy of vibration and clean it out, replacing the old feelings with those of positivity which will change into a feeling of happiness. And once you are vibrating that happiness out into the Universe, the Universe will match that vibration and send back the positive experiences, like good health or more money. It opens that positive flow.

You do not need to be positive 100 percent of the time; being 51 percent positive on a daily basis is enough to tip the scale. Lean towards the positive more of the time, knowing that the Universe responds to our thinking. We want to be in positive vibrational harmony for our good to come to us.

"Life is a state of consciousness."

—Emmet Fox

Don't Be Afraid of Your Own Power

Now that you know that you have the power to create your own reality, one question that may come up after you have spent mental energy on negativity is, "How do I stop it?" Here are three strategies:

One: Stop and ask yourself what you like to do in your spare time. What is your hobby? For example, let's say you like to play board games, do puzzles, garden, sing, or paint. Distract yourself from the negativity and just do what's fun for you. That will stop that negative energy because you are distracting yourself from it; instead find something that's fun and brings you joy. Now your attention is starting to shift.

Two: What if you don't have any hobbies or you are out somewhere and have this negative feeling? How do you make a shift there?

In a relaxed state of mind, let the answer come to you. This is when you relax and gently ask your Inner Being for guidance. We all have an Inner Being which guides us. You simply ask your Inner Being, "How can I feel better? I want to feel better. How can I get over this? How can I feel more positive?"

A thought will come to your mind. You will feel an inner voice talking to you, saying, "This is the way." It's the little voice inside of you; it's a feeling you'll pick up. It cancels all the negativity for you. Whatever unhappiness or frustration you're feeling fades away. Once you practice and experience it, you will know.

Keep in mind that when you ask your Inner Being for an answer, you have to feel at peace and allow the answer to come. But if you're in frustration of any kind, you will block the answer. Similarly, if a dear friend is calling you, but you're busy talking on that phone line, the call cannot come through. Your frustration or worry is like the blockage of the phone call. The phone line has to be clear to receive the call; you need to get yourself to feeling relaxed and having the assurance that the answer always comes when you ask.

Three: Another way to get back into alignment is to pick up an uplifting book and read a few passages. Focus on the positive message in the book and not on your problems or frustration or negative feelings. Self-help books are good for this. Read a few pages to shift your energy to the positive.

Awakening to the Law

I first learned about this Universal Law back in 2008 when Oprah was talking about the book, *The Secret,* by Rhonda Byrne. That's when I felt the upliftment, like a renewal. My first thought was, *Wow, is this for real? It sounds too good to be true.* Since then, I have studied and discovered a lot more. Over the past ten years, I have been reading every day. I study the masters from the late 1800s to early 1900s like Neville Goddard, Florence Scovel Shinn, Ralph Waldorf Emerson, Thomas Troward, and Phineas Quimby. They provided pure information that is powerful.

After learning more about the Laws of the Universe, I realized that I had been applying it in my life unconsciously. When you are not aware of it, the experience can be hit or miss. If you don't know the Laws of the Universe, you go through life stumbling around and drifting with the wind. When you have no idea that you are the creator of your own life, you're happy when good things happen and react negatively when awful things happen; you do not realize how things happened the way they did. When you understand it, you create deliberately and not by default. We are all the attractors of our experiences.

But now, I understand; I know exactly what I did, and I've always used my Inner Being without knowing the Law of Attraction. Since I was a kid, it was like a guardian angel. So I've always made use of that, unconsciously. But of course it's good to use it on purpose.

My unconscious example of applying the Law before I really understood it came early in my marriage nearly three decades ago. I had four miscarriages, and the fourth miscarriage was a stillbirth. I was pregnant for five months and the baby died. They had to induce labor; I went through the labor pains without a baby because it died inside.

After that fourth miscarriage, I got pregnant again. Early in my pregnancy, I found an adorable yellow baby jumpsuit in the size of a two-month-old baby. I bought it and hung it in my closet where it was visible as I walked down my hallway. Each day, several times a day, I would see the baby jumpsuit hanging in my closet and I would stop to hug it as if my baby were in it. I loved the jumpsuit so much. I felt the feelings as if my baby were wearing it. I did so because it made me feel good. Feeling good is key. That pure desire made it manifest into actuality—the feeling of the wish fulfilled. I didn't do it to make it manifest; I did it for the good feeling. And when you do something for the feeling, that's how you manifest.

Finally, when my baby was born, I actually lived that feeling in real life with my baby in that jumpsuit. I even had a video recording of him when he fit into that jumpsuit. I thought that was so powerful. I thought if anyone wanted to have a baby and they have this problem, they could just do the same thing, and it would change their life. It was so thrilling. It was such a miracle how it manifested.

Think about that. I had had four miscarriages already. I thought, *Oh I want to have a baby.* I found this jumpsuit and I got pregnant, and I was able to keep the baby because of my desire to have a baby. I used the jumpsuit as an object to magnify the feeling as if I were living that reality. The Universe had to match with my desire and brought it to pass.

I had no more miscarriages after I did that visualization. I was able to have two perfect babies, and no matter what difficulty I went through, that baby had to live and survive and wear that jumpsuit. Talk about feeling the feelings of the wish fulfilled: miraculous.

"Imagination creates reality."

—Neville Goddard

Manifesting a House

I lived in a fairly new home that was lovely, but I desired a more elegant home with a sweeping overlook from the upstairs. Several months later, we went and looked at the construction plans for a new home that we intended to buy for members of our family. It was larger and had many elegant features, but I could only see this in the plans, not a true model of the home. It was not built yet. The plans said it had certain features and an upstairs railing, but the descriptions didn't mean much to me in the drawing plan.

We had the house built. It had a granny unit and plenty of room for our family members. But when the relatives went to see it, they did not want it. They felt it was too elegant for them. As it turned out, the newer house had exactly what I had envisioned before we looked at these model homes. We did not plan to move at the time. We were just in our own home for less than two years and it had many upgrades. But now we had two houses and two mortgages, but I did not want to rent the newer house out. I had to decide what to do with each of the homes.

We paid two mortgages for a couple of months before I made the decision on which house to live in. Both homes were perfect; but the newer one had a better neighborhood and location. Once I made that decision to move into the newer home and sell the other home, we put it up for sale and made a good profit. We ended up moving into this newer house. I had imagined it in my mind, and because of the Law of Attraction, it had to manifest to match my vision. My vision and my desire for this certain house made the other person not want to move in. It had to be mine because I had wanted it.

This not only shows the Universal Laws in action, but it shows the abundance of the Universe. There is no need for a scarcity mentality. When you have a scarcity mentality, you might think, "If I get what I want, that means somebody else isn't getting what they want." But the house is an example of how someone else chose not to accept it, and it became available for me rather than being taken from somebody else in order for me to have it. That's not the way the Law works. There's abundance in the Universe. And in this case, it wasn't what they wanted, but it was what I wanted. It's beautiful how it manifested like that. I didn't have to fight for it. It was just given to me because I had envisioned it. It was just handed to me. And then on top of that, I sold my other home at a great profit.

If you visualize it and feel it and want it, it's yours; other people will not want it. There is no competition. So relax and focus on the wishes you want to have fulfilled.

Once you decide on what you want, then the Universe puts your desire into place for you. It's with indecision that you don't get it. This house is an example. Once I knew what I wanted, I decided, and then I moved forward with ease.

If you visualize it and feel it and want it, it's yours.

Following Your Guidance

All of us are confused sometimes and want to go about making the right decisions. When that happens, realize that you have an Inner Guidance which will lead you and direct you. You will know this as an intense inner feeling—a hunch leading you to the right place in the right time, causing you to say the right words and guide you in the right path.

I frequently practice turning to my Inner Being to guide me. I use it often. I ask for it. I learned how to trust it because it's always given me the right decision. A lot of people would turn outside to their friends or to other people to help them make a decision. And it's not the right decision for you. It might be the right one for them. But you have your own guidance that is looking out for you and showing what is best for you. Nobody else from the outside can do that.

Are there times when others can give you good advice and direction? Yes, but you need to get in agreement with your Inner

Being. The answer can come through others. But that's when the emotion comes in and you'll feel like, yes, it's the right choice. If it's not, you will feel a no, it's the wrong one.

In asking for answers, put yourself in a relaxed, positive state, and then ask for the right answer. Say to yourself, "Infinite Intelligence within me, give me the right idea," for whatever problem you need to solve. Then, feel confident that the answer is revealed to you and give thanks for it.

How do you know when it's the right choice to make, even after you ask?

You will receive a correct answer only when you ask while feeling positive emotion. If you are in frustration or worry or have any kind of resistant emotion, you won't get a clear answer. You will know by the way you feel, which is an indication of whether you are in alignment or not.

This happened to me. I was asking for a certain answer, and when it came it wasn't right. I thought, *Why didn't I get the right answer?* Later that evening, I realized that I wasn't feeling relaxed. I was frustrated and anxious and wasn't aware of my emotions.

So, regardless of whether you are in a good place about what you're asking, if there are other concerns or other confusion about other topics, then you can still have that unclarity. You can still have a confused result because of your mixed emotions at that point.

Rhonda Byrne's book, *The Secret,* said you have to desire something to receive it; you have to be hungry for it. You have to want it before you get it. I thought, *Okay, I read the book. I used it. I want something. I really want it. How come I didn't get it?* This question wasn't answered in *The Secret*. But it was a good start for someone who's just learning.

I learned later that desire without resistance brings it into manifestation.

Now, I use my Inner Guidance too. I would receive an inner voice; it is an experience of clairaudience.

For instance, one time my husband was driving us home after a party and he was going over the speed limit. The voices inside told me, "Tell him to slow down. There's a cop around the bend." But I didn't say anything to him.

All of a sudden, a cop was right behind us and told my husband to pull over. He had to get out and deal with the officer for over fifteen minutes.

I said to myself, "Oh my God, I didn't even tell him. The voice told me to tell him, but I didn't."

After that incident, I learned to always pay attention to my intuition.

Faith through the Fog

I want to share another driving example from several years ago.

I was enjoying an event at a friend's house where we were doing a singing gig. When we finally decided to go home, it was after one in the morning. Before we left, I went to the restroom. In the hallway, my friend had a decorative plaque that said, "I am with you." I get chills as I write this.

So, I saw this plaque and read it, and I felt a sense of empowering protection and security.

My husband and I headed out on our three-hour drive home. It was wintertime. It wasn't raining, but it was really foggy. Once we got onto the freeway, we couldn't even see the road. We were driving a truck and could only see up to the hood. We couldn't see the road because the fog was so thick. How can you drive when you only see the hood?

We were able to turn onto another route where it had a larger freeway with other commuters and was more visible. It was still foggy, but better here than there. After we exited, there was just one car ahead of us. It was helping us to see; it was guiding us the whole time. When driving became more visible, the other car turned off the road; it turned when we got to a visible place. We were able to drive a clear path after that. So we were guided when we couldn't see and were able to exit before it was too late onto another road. Had we gone a bit further on that first route, we would have missed the turnoff and would have had no choice but to keep driving in that dense fog. Once we exited, we were guided by this angel to our house three hours away.

When we arrived home safely, I was reminded of that plaque that said, "I am with you."

Tips and Actions

1. Now that you know your thoughts, together with your feelings, create your reality, catch any negative feelings early and snap out of the mood by thinking of something positive. Find a good feeling or happy moment from your past and enjoy the feeling of it again. Allow the good feeling to take precedence. Reread this chapter to remind you of your power.

2. Write down a few happy moments that stir up happy feelings in you. Then look at that list and replay it in your mind whenever you need to (like when you want to have a pity party). If you retrace those past happy feelings for a few minutes, you will find more happy feelings to feel. And positive experiences will manifest the next day (or soon thereafter) to match that happy feeling.

3. When you run into a problem or decision point, ask the Universe in a relaxed state of mind, "Show me the right way. I want to make the right decision." With faith and confidence, you will receive an answer. Relaxation is important. When you have a thought or idea and it feels good to you, act on it.

PART II

HOW DISEASE IS CREATED IN THE BODY

*"Even though the body appears to be material, it is not.
In the deeper reality, your body is a field of energy,
transformation, and intelligence."*

—Deepak Chopra

Any discomfort in the body was created from negative emotions. If a person experienced an illness of any kind, it was all in the energy or vibration in the person's mind. This energy was brought into the body. A person with a harmonious mind, who felt content most of the time, would not encounter physical illness. So before any disease manifests in a person's body, it was first created in their mind. They do not have to think of a certain disease to attract it, but worry or fear or resentment or any negative emotion will manifest in the body in time. They would first have to cancel out those negative emotions or neutralize them before they could get a complete or permanent healing. They cannot say, "I want a healing," and still hold on to the fear or the worry or the grudges. So, if they were upset with another person, they would need to let go of the negative feelings—to forgive and forget and bless the person—and then move on. Once the negative emotion is gone, then you can have a complete healing.

Sometimes a person experiences a manifested condition in the body without knowing consciously what happened or how it came about. Regardless, if a person experiences an illness, it is from past thinking that created it. What you were thinking and feeling in the past brought it forward; it didn't just happen by chance.

We build in thought the conditions that later will
come into manifestation on the physical plane.

—Emmet Fox

Many people do not realize that negative emotion causes illness and physical discord. They blame it on food, like the type of vegetables or meat they eat. They mainly focus on what they eat. They are not aware that it's the mind, it's the thoughts, that cause illness. They think that it is because of what they ate that they had cancer. But no, it's your thoughts every day—that discordant thinking that causes those illnesses. If you have constantly destructive thoughts, what you eat does not help you in any way. Outer action will not affect inner action. But when a person's mind is right, they are being guided to eat the right food. And because their thinking is right, everything else takes care of itself.

It is not the wrong nutrition that causes disease. We have all known people who had the healthiest food and a good diet and still came down with diseases. You are what you mentally eat. What you eat physically, psychologically, and spiritually matters. If you absorb and digest happiness, joy, and success, you will attract and experience these in your life. Fear, thoughts of worry, critical thoughts, and angry, hateful thoughts are foods of sickness and misery. And foods of health are the ones mentioned before: happiness, joy, optimism, and other positive emotions. This is why we need to feed our mind the right mental nutrition. If you have jealousy and anger, your food may become poisonous. Food for the body is important, but your mental and spiritual diet is of greater importance. So now you can choose the right foods for your mind.

Don't retain resentment, hate, or anger. A great philosopher told a story of a man who was a specialist on nutrition but suffered an ulcer. His doctor gave him a special diet, but the ulcer worsened. It turns out that every time he read the paper, he was angry about the government and their actions. He was angry by this all the time. When you have negative energy all the time, you have to change your mental and emotional diet. So, it is not the food you eat, but the food you feed your mind that deteriorates the body. Food for our body is important, but the food for our mental and spiritual health is more important.

The Power of Forgiveness

You must get rid of all sense of resentment and hostility. You must change your state of mind until it's in harmony and at peace within yourself, and you have positive goodwill towards everyone. You have to forgive others or you cannot make any improvement. It's not easy to forgive people who have hurt you so deeply or injured or deceived you. You might say, "It's impossible; I cannot forgive them," but there is no escape from this situation but to forgive. No matter how deeply we may have been injured or how terribly we have suffered, it must be done.

Setting others free means setting yourself free, because resentment is really a form of attachment. When you hold resentment against anyone, you are bound to that person by a cosmic link—a *mental chain*. You are *cosmically tied* to the thing you hate. The person you most dislike is the very one to whom you are *attaching* yourself by a hook that is stronger than steel. Is this what you wish? Is this the condition in which you desire to go on living?

Remember, you *belong* to the thing with which you are linked in thought; if that tie continues, the person you resent will be drawn again into your life, perhaps to work further destruction. Do you think that you can afford this? Nobody can afford such a thing. You must *cut all* such ties by an act of *forgiveness*. You must let the person loose and let him or her go. By forgiveness, you set yourself *free*, and you save your soul.

The technique of forgiveness is simple, and not difficult to manage when you understand how. What is extremely important is the willingness to forgive; when you have the desire to forgive a person, the greater part of the work is already done.

The method of forgiving is this:

1. Go to a quiet place and get into a relaxed state.
2. Then say, "I fully and freely forgive (mentioning the person's name). I loosen him and let him go. He is now free, and I am free too. I wish him well in all phases of his life. That incident is finished. We are all free. I give thanks."
3. Then go about your day.

Afterward, whenever the memory of the person happens to come into your mind, bless the person and dismiss the thought. Do this as many times as the thought may come up. After a few days, it will return less and less often, until you forget it altogether. Eventually, all the anger and resentment will disappear, and you are both free. Your forgiveness is complete. You will experience a joyful realization of the ideal manifestation.

Making a Positive Change

We are here living in this world with a life of contrast between wanted and unwanted things. We experience both positive and negative situations, but you now know that we can create better situations and better life experiences. We can do that with our thoughts. We can change our life circumstances to what we want using our minds. This is where the power lies. We have the potential to alter our lives. We are given minds to think and to create our lives the way we desire.

*Human beings can alter their lives by
altering their attitudes of mind.*

—William James, The Father of Psychology

We can change our bodies to healthy conditions by having more pleasant thoughts. Care about feeling good. You don't need to be always feeling good or always having only positive emotion, but be aware when you are in alignment and when you are not. Choose a thought on purpose. Be deliberate about it.

We can use our imaginations to create what we want. We're not stuck with the undesirable present condition. When you understand how the Universe operates, you have peace of mind and security. You are not concerned with any unwanted condition in your life because you know you can change it. This is empowering.

What If?

What if you discover a pain, but at the time of discovery, you are not in a negative state?

Your past unconscious thinking or negative thoughts brought on that pain; that's how it manifests in that condition. You must have thought of some worries yesterday, last month, or a couple of weeks ago that you're not aware of, because when you have that stagnate energy within yourself, it manifests as pain. There is always a cause behind every effect. When you look back, you will realize this and say, "Oh my goodness, I was worried about this and that recently." Let me give you an illustration.

A friend of mine called me a few weeks ago saying she had cut her hand badly and had to go to the emergency room. She was simply taking out the trash. The metal lid cut through her skin when she grabbed it and cut the vein on her thumb. She was bleeding profusely. I explained to her that she must have been concerned or worried about something prior to this cutting. She had to have some discord in her mind, some concern, or some worry before that.

She told me she was worried about taking a trip that made her anxious. She was worried about the flight, and she didn't feel like going. She had anxiety. That was about three or four days before the accident. I then explained that she needed to find a way to have peace of mind and to get rid of all the worry, because this time it was a cut on her hand; it may be serious, but something worse could happen if she continued to have negative thoughts. She needed to pivot to a different emotion, or to find a better feeling thought, and to release the worry or anxiety and all the concerns.

She admitted that she was worried, and that by the Law of Attraction she had attracted the condition, which was the manifestation of the emotional discord. When she realized what the cause was, she understood how to change it.

But if you blame someone else for your problem, you are not taking that power for yourself. You're giving your power away. Now, when you know how the situation came about, you can fix it and turn it around and create a pleasant experience. Never blame anything or anyone else; it's always a person's own attraction. But knowing that you can change it is where you have the power.

One of my longtime friends had a serious, third-degree, burn from cooking. She was frying meat and the oil made a big splash onto her face, eyelid, chest, and a few other spots. Her skin came off in those areas hit by the hot oil. She iced the places that she could get to, especially on the face, for many hours until the burnt sensation eased away.

She called me, frantically, that evening explaining the incident. She was also concerned because she had a wedding to attend the next day.

I tried to soothe her and calm her down. I told her to keep icing it until the burned sensation goes away, then told her to use Neosporin® to help relieve the pain.

She asked me, "Why did that happened to me?"

I questioned her, "Was there something that bothered you recently?"

I asked her to reflect back how she was feeling.

She said, "A few days ago I was so angry at one of my customers; she was rude and obnoxious."

Her intense anger had attracted to her that situation. That negative emotion brought about the burns. She has knowledge of the Laws of the Universe. If she had been aware of the unpleasant emotions and caught them early, she would have neutralized them and never experienced the burns.

I told her that our bodies have the ability to heal themselves. They can repair and give us new skin. In the meantime, I suggested that she find a picture of herself that she likes, especially a photo that visibly shows her pretty face, and place it where she could see it all the time (such as her bathroom mirror).

She took my suggestion. She looked at the picture often during the day and evening and felt the feeling of her face being renewed to its original skin again. Within about three days, those areas where she had iced intensely had peeled off. The burned skin had peeled off.

In a few months' time, they completely healed. All the scars faded away as if she had never been burned, giving her new fresh skin. It was as if nothing had happened. Normally, there tends to be some type of scar from a third-degree burn. But by working with this principle, her skin was made new.

Looking at the picture she had placed on the mirror, every day, and feeling the reality and the naturalness of the renewed skin like the photo had brought it to pass.

What we feel and imagine, we attract. It is Law!

What about Chronic Pain?

I have been asked about people who have issues like fibromyalgia or joint disease, arthritis, or chronic pain. How can they reconcile that? They'll say, "Well, I've had this for fifteen years...." They see it as pervasive, as long term, and as theirs. They are told there's nothing they can do about it. What do you tell somebody who's experienced something for a long time, so long that they may not be able to track their source of negativity? Can they just release whatever negativity there is even if they don't know that that's what led to their manifestation?

One of the reasons for chronic pain: Believing that it's hereditary.

When the parents have the illness, the child believes that it was passed on to them. That's a false belief, and it must be unraveled.

Another reason for chronic pain: Feeling a sense of guilt.

They feel that they must be punished for wrongdoing unto another from many years ago. It's self-condemnation. To neutralize that belief, you have to realize that you're not that same person anymore. You're condemning an innocent person.

A third reason for chronic pain: Feeling of resistance within oneself.

You should not entertain in your mind negative thoughts such as resentment, hate, jealously, hostility, or anger. When you allow negative energy to build up inside you, it has an effect on you.

When you are in physical pain, it's hard not to focus on it. First of all, you must be at peace with where you are, no matter how uncomfortable it is. Unless you are feeling some sense of ease with where you are, you cannot get to a better place. Because if your attention is focused on what is wrong and on all those feelings of discomfort, it's not possible to get to the place you want to be from that negative emotion—they are opposing vibrations. It's a process of thinking. You have to use the power of your mind to find a feeling place of relief from the pain. In feeling hopeful and feeling the essence of comfort, you'll be guided towards a solution. The ideas will occur to you, and you'll end up finding remedies to help with the cure.

Your cells have intelligent consciousness. They are requesting the healing that is being given, and if you are not in resistant thought, then you will receive a healing.

Don't Complain about the Pain

I met a friend a year ago, and she is constantly complaining about her health. Her condition is serious, but she's always talking about it. She's always mentioning to people that she's ill, she can't do this, she can't eat that, because it will aggravate her condition. All I hear her talk about is her ailment. She always brings it up. She'll say she has this pain or that problem like she owns it. I suggested that she not talk about her ailment. Don't go around constantly talking about it.

When you keep looking at the manifested condition and giving it attention, you're keeping it alive. Your attention to anything not wanted activates the vibration of it and holds you to it longer.

Allow your mind to focus on the solution of wellness and you will cause your energy to shift into healing. Everything is about energy flow, and the cause of illness is vibrational. Direct your attention to what is wanted.

Childhood Conditions and Attracting What You Think About

I am often asked how this works with somebody who has had a physical condition for a long time. They didn't have any understanding of the laws of the universe at that time, so how does someone turn something like that around?

Let's take my daughter as an example. She's the only one who wears glasses in the family. She still does. In her case, early in grade school, she started thinking, *Oh, I wanna wear glasses. I think glasses are cool.*

But her eyes were fine at the time. Yet, her desire was to wear glasses. I didn't notice at the time. She told me years later that she wanted it. That's why she needs them now. So, now, I can tell her the process of what to do to turn it around. But as a child, she was too young to understand.

Whether a person thinks on purpose or by default, the Universe receives the impression of the thought and brings it in as a condition. In my daughter's case, she desired the glasses until she attracted the need for them. In my own case, I had to wear glasses in junior high school through high school. I was nearsighted and wore glasses for four years.

I did not know of the Law of Attraction yet. I was just a kid under sixteen. But unconsciously, I was saying to myself, I want to improve my eyesight. I want to have clear vision. So four or so years later, I went to the DMV because they needed to recheck my eyesight for my license renewal. Back then, when you wore glasses, they had you read the board to test your vision, and they noted on your license that you have corrective lenses. But before I went in there, I consciously was thinking, I want to see it clearly.

And then the tester said, "Why don't you try it without your glasses?" My desire caused her to say that.

I said, "Oh, okay, let me try without my glasses."

And I found out that I could read everything just fine. Despite wearing glasses four or five years prior. After that, my license didn't say I wore corrective lenses anymore. I didn't need glasses anymore.

It was a miracle, right?

I still don't wear glasses. So my experience was opposite of my daughter's because I was saying "I want to have good eyesight to see clearly without glasses," and it caused a person to say, "take off your glasses and read without them."

You can tell yourself, "Infinite Intelligence is within me. God within me sees clearly and reads through me." That power within you will cause you to create that better vision. You are one with an Inner Being or Infinite Intelligence and Infinite Intelligence can see clearly.

Claim it in Like Shinn

Florence Scovel Shinn was one of the great teachers and authors from the 1920s. She was helping a woman who wanted to have clear eyes and vision, but the woman was making the wrong statement.

The woman said, "I want to lose my glasses. I want to get rid of my glasses." The statement wasn't clear, and she kept losing her glasses.

She actually wanted to get rid of the need to wear glasses and to have clear eyes, but because she said, "I want to lose my glasses," she kept misplacing her glasses every day.

So Florence finally said, "You have to say, 'I want to have clear vision.' And you tell yourself that every day until it becomes a habit. And then the Inner Being comes through and eventually you get your clear vision."

That's how you state it—you have to be precise. Yes, the eyes can be improved by making that statement and by *believing* it and by *knowing* that Infinite Intelligence can see through you clearly. But you have to be clear about what you want.

Striking a Balance

How do you balance focusing on something you want to correct and not putting energy into its incorrectness? By putting energy on the correctness and not putting energy in its incorrectness. By only giving your attention to what you desire. Putting your attention on what is going well.

A wise teacher taught these lines:

When you have only one thing going right and the other ninety-nine going wrong, and you focus on the ONE that is going right, then the other ninety-nine will all be well.

On the other hand, when you have only one thing going wrong and the ninety-nine are going right and you focus on that ONE that is going wrong, the other ninety-nine will all be rotten too.

You see, it's all in the power of focus. What we give attention to makes it grow, because this is a universe of attraction. Our thought has a frequency. This is tremendously important to realize.

We also strike a balance by not using effort to correct anything. Trying to correct something puts the emphasis on what is wrong, and then what is wrong will be attracted. When the focus is not to think of something, you're thinking about it.

By turning your attention to what feels pleasant to you, you are making a shift in a different direction.

Be optimistic

Have faith

Expect wellness

Instead of looking at the unwanted manifestation, we must turn our attention to the desire of being well, which will cause us to have a soothing feeling. It's a feeling of relief. And then that positive emotion will cause us to attract the solution for the cure.

Then the doctor will say, "Let's do this," and we'll feel that it's the right decision.

My Long-term Battle with Pain

I had pain for over ten years. My OB/GYN recommended that I get a hysterectomy to remove the uterus and get rid of the pain. I didn't want to go through surgery. I thought to myself, "There has to be another solution."

Uterine fibroids caused the pain to be unbearable. Even taking pills didn't help. It was like going through childbirth every month, but without a baby. When it came on, it disrupted my whole life. It got to the point that I couldn't do anything: I couldn't go to work, and I had to call and cancel all my client appointments every month at the salon.

Finally, I came across a tea for fibroid healing. I read their customers' testimonials: women who had fibroids for many years whose OB doctors recommended they get a hysterectomy to remove the uterus, but they didn't want to take that suggestion. They found this remedy instead of going through surgery and became completely healed by taking this tea. After reading all about those wonderful statements, I was extremely excited and was filled with joy. I thought to myself, "That's it! That's the solution!"

I ordered it. Within a month of taking the fibroid tea, when my next cycle came, I didn't feel any pain at all. It was such a relief. Pain-free after so many years. It's a miracle! I'm completely healed!

I intuitively felt that there was another solution to this rather than surgery to remove the uterus. My feeling guided me towards this route and I followed it. It brought me to the right path.

What We Choose to Think Can Impact Others

We are living in a vibrational universe. Every cell has the ability to transmit and receive thought. Leaving your mind open to suggestion and public opinion will have an impact. Doctors have concluded that illness is hereditary, because the cells of the infant were communicating with the cells of the sick parent's body or with their fearful thoughts. Babies cannot think for themselves. So when an infant grows up in the family with a sick parent, the infant picks it up vibrationally and telepathically.

There is great power in decision. Decide not to let the experiences of other people or their evidence of physical disease or poverty affect your experience. Their evidence has nothing to do with yours. They attract their own experiences through their thoughts and beliefs. You have control over your own experience. It is only a matter of you deciding what you want and knowing the process that will bring it into your experience.

For example, when you love someone, you transmit that energy with another. The same is true with hatred for someone; you communicate that through your energy, and not with words.

So if a baby is sick, you can heal the baby and teach those around the baby to think in a positive, constructive way, radiating harmonious thoughts to have the baby permanently healed.

Here's an illustration of how infants pick up parents' energy. Babies can't talk or decide for themselves. When my daughter was a baby of five to six months, she ran a really high fever. The doctor told me to give her medicine, but the fever would not go down after several doses. I was so worried. I didn't realize how parents affected babies' health.

My husband and I had been in an intense argument and were angry at one another. We were terribly agitated and emotionally disturbed. This disturbed feeling was communicated telepathically to the baby and she got ill. Children are controlled by the dominant mental atmosphere of the people around them. The fever of the baby was caused by the anger and rage of the parents, which was vibrationally felt by the baby and expressed as a high fever. When the situation cleared, when we both were no longer feverish or angry at each other, the baby's fever went away.

Tips and Actions

1. Every disease was first created in the mind. We have to feed our mind the right mental nutrition.
2. Don't talk about your ailment; that will only keep it alive. Direct your mind to the solution of healing.
3. It's all mental work. Pay attention to your emotions. Catch it early, because a negative feeling will attract a negative situation which could turn into a health issue.
4. Do something fun; find something to feel good about.
5. You only need 51 percent of good energy to tip the balance or scale to create a positive outcome.
6. Be mindful of how your energy can impact others, including your children. Radiate harmonious positive energy and it will be received by those around you.
7. Focus your attention on what is going right and then everything else will take care of itself.
8. Forgiving others means setting yourself free.
9. If in pain or discomfort, use the power of your mind to find a feeling of relief.
10. Nothing happens in the body except it first takes place in the mind. A healthy mind produces a healthy body.

PART III

USING THE MIND IN THE HEALING PROCESS

"We've in fact conditioned ourselves to believe all sorts of things that aren't necessarily true—and many of these things are having a negative impact on our health and happiness."

—Dr. Joe Dispenza

Boosting the Belief of Healing

True faith in healing is the understanding of how your mind operates. A healing Presence is in us and flows through us. You have to be conscious of its existence to have it working for you. It has to work through you, which means it happens through your belief for the healing to be effective.

Let me share an example with my daughter. As an early teenager, she was going through an abnormal menstrual cycle. The cycle would start and stop, only to have it come back again. This went on for a few weeks. She may have been losing too much blood in the process, which can be a concern. She was scared and panicky. She came to me for help.

As a mom, I wanted to help soothe the situation. I was trying to think of an effective way to help her. I wanted to say the right words. I was trying to think of a way to get her to a feeling of belief. Then a light bulb came on in my head! I remembered that I was given red woven thread bracelets by Buddhist monks some time ago that I had kept in my nightstand. At the time, the monk had given me four thread bracelets for my family: for me, my husband, my son, and my daughter. These bracelets are believed by many to have healing powers and bring abundance of wealth. I took one bracelet from my drawer and tied it on her wrist, telling her,

"This bracelet I received from a monk has healing power in it. Wearing it will heal you of this condition."

She felt a sense of soothing, and that night she went to bed feeling relaxed with a sense of calmness and comfort.

Within the next day her symptom had improved, and her health became normal. She was cured from the condition.

What I did was to get her to believe that the thread bracelet had healing power. She believed me; I implanted that belief in her. Her deeper mind took that belief and caused a healing.

**When your mind moves from fear to
faith you receive a healing.**

What you believe comes to pass.

The true faith of healing is based on the knowledge of how our minds operate. It is specifically directed. Blind faith is allowing healing to happen without understanding the forces involved. Blind faith is what my daughter had. It wasn't the thread bracelet that healed her, it was the belief. In any case, whatever you believe comes to pass. Whatever condition she had at the time healed the next day. It is moving from fear to faith that opened the door to healing.

Napoleon Hill's son, Blair, was born without ears. His parents constantly told him that he could still hear, and he believed this without questioning the physical limitation of it, and he began to hear despite having no ears.

Exercising True Faith

I know the working power of our minds. I know that the healing power is within me; I claim it and know it will heal me, because it is a servant of my thoughts and my will.

I encourage you to recognize your healing power. True spirit is the healer. Creative intelligence in the universe performs the magnificent act throughout your consciousness. That is why you have control to believe.

Healing comes through your consciousness. You have to *believe* for this power to work for you. It can't just happen to you; it can only do *for* you what it does *through* you. It flows through that thought pattern. Heal the vibrational discord first, then it will flow through new thought patterns and heal your body. If you don't acknowledge it or believe it, it won't happen for you. It is that invisible wall. Don't have belief? Healing can't come to you. The same is true for money. If you say you can't make that much money, and you believe it, money will stop coming to you. If you know you can make more money, you will receive more money.

Another example: three people go to the beach, each with a pail. One has a small bucket, another a medium bucket, and the third carries a large bucket. They all have different sized portions that they bring home. Their bucket size represents their consciousness. They can only have what their consciousness can conceive, no more and no less.

Building true faith is like building muscle—it takes practice to exercise that faith. Look around in your environment. You see others who have accomplished so much. Realize that you have the same ability; you just have to learn how to use it. We are all God's children with the same capacity. It is not assigned to you by fate; it is what you make of it. That same power in the universe is given to everyone. We can achieve our goals and desires and heal our bodies using the power of our minds by learning the Universal Law and how it operates, and by working in harmony with it.

Learning to Work with Your Inner Being

We all have an Inner Being. You can call it God, Infinite Intelligence, nature, life principle, or your Higher Self; that is up to you. We can contact this Infinite Presence within us with our thoughts. To receive help, create a solution, or have anything work for you, you have to be in conscious awareness of this Being. You have to give it recognition. That is the meaning of contact with our thoughts. For instance, a man I met would say, "I don't have God within me. I don't have an Inner Being."

So when he says he doesn't have an Inner Being, it's as if he is shutting it out.

Everyone has an Inner Guidance. It lies dormant if you are not aware of this great power. When you become conscious of it and give it recognition, it awakens.

Whenever you need to solve any problem or call on it for help, first get into a relaxed state of mind and then say, "Infinite Intelligence give me the answer I need for this problem," or whatever it is you need to know.

Many years ago I had a tenant who couldn't pay rent for eight months. He had a steady job, but he got ill and couldn't return to work, so he fell behind on his rent. Everyone else who knew of the situation told me to kick him out. I didn't have the heart to evict him. I felt so much sympathy for him. If I kicked him out, he would have ended up on the street.

I wanted so much to receive the rent from him. Then I remembered Florence Shinn's book that I'd read some years prior. She said, "There is a supply for every demand."

I then gathered my thoughts together and got into a relaxed mode. I said, "Infinite Intelligence, open the way for my tenant to receive the funds he needs. I give thanks. It now manifests under grace in a perfect way."

After meditating in this way I felt an inner peace, knowing my prayer would be answered.

I then went about my business, doing my daily living, and forgetting about the problem. I was not disturbed about the issue. Instead, I was feeling at ease and at peace with the situation.

When I saw my tenant approximately a week later, he told me, "I applied for rental assistance, and I should be getting money from the time I stopped working, which is close to a year."

I was so delighted; it was like music to my ears. I said to him, "That is so awesome!"

He continued, saying, "I think I owe you about a million dollars now." He said it jokingly, because the amount was so much.

A short time afterward, he received the rental assistance and paid every penny he owed me.

My prayer was answered in the way I desired!

Once you ask, be at peace. Know that you will receive a response. Put the matter out of your mind and go about your business. When you least expect it, the answer will flash in your mind. You will get an overpowering hunch, or a feeling that you are being guided to do the right thing. It may give the answer in a dream. It might come in an intuition or from a person. Whichever way it comes, you will recognize that it's the right solution. You will feel inspired to act.

It takes practice, but once you experience it, you'll know how it works. That sense of knowing is powerful!

Your Inner Being Can Use Various Channels

Around eight years ago, I was getting discoloration on my face. I had pigmented, dark spots on both cheeks. It was so dark and it kind of scared me. I wondered, *What's going on? Why is my skin pigmented when I used to have a clear and beautiful complexion?*

So I asked my Inner Being, "How can I clear this? And what causes it?" It was so dark; very noticeable. So I asked how it came about.

That night I had a dream. In my dream, a best friend told me, "You know, I went to a fortune teller, a person who reads the future, and he said that you should stay away from liquor because the liquor caused your pigmentation."

And I woke up in a shock: that was it! A couple of evenings before, I was drinking a few shots, and had never had that large amount before. The dark spots developed shortly after that. I was shown the way it came about.

We have many friends and are always having get togethers. I rarely drink alcohol, but once in a while I will take a few sips to raise a toast with friends. Since I received the answer to the cause, I stayed away from that completely. So my complexion's been clear.

Your subjective mind only uses a person whom you love and admire (such as my best friend) in your dream state. It would not send someone you dislike.

The Power of Imagination

Imagination is the faculty of image making; it has the power to project and create your ideas. Imagination is a powerful instrument used by scientists, physicists, inventors, poets, mystics, and artists—all the people whom we ever considered to be great. They understand the amazing and miraculous power of mental imaging.

Before anything happens or shows up in our lives, we first have to give it thought and have it in our consciousness before it manifests. This is why imagination is so important.

Imagination rules the world.

—Napoleon Bonaparte

For people who are not physically mobile, but who desire to be able to walk in a normal, natural way:

Relax in a quiet place for ten to fifteen minutes per day. Imagine yourself doing the things you used to do *before* the injury. If you like gardening, actually feel yourself working in the garden. If you like skiing, feel the wind on your cheeks as you're swishing down the slopes. Or go swimming, or climbing mountains, or do any hobbies and activities you enjoy doing. Feel the naturalness of it; get into the spirit of performing the activity.

Notice that it's not just seeing yourself as an illusion projected outside yourself, looking from distance. You don't just see it in your mind, you *feel* yourself doing it.

You can mentally hear your doctor telling you, "It's a miracle! You are completely well." Rejoice in hearing and feeling the good news.

You want to actually feel the realness of it. Get in that mental state of actualizing the activity. Do this without effort—don't force yourself, don't try too hard. You're not trying to make it happen. You want to do for the pleasure of it, because it makes you feel good.

This is when the magic happens.

It is vitally important to imagine before bed. Imagine that you are *now* physically well and are doing your desired activity before falling to sleep. Feel satisfied and happy about your imaginary experience. Then your Subjective Mind, which is your deeper mind where the healing power is, will respond to your imagery and feeling, and the healing takes place.

Be Aware

Keep this in mind: if you are fearful or worried, you're imagining in a negative direction. It's faith upside-down. It's believing in the wrong thing. When you're dwelling on a negative situation, such as worry about your health or a lack of money, it is using your imagination in a destructive way.

The way you can tell which direction you're heading is if you're feeling good or feeling bad as you're thinking the thought. If your emotion is not good, then redirect your thought, because emotion follows thought, and what we imagine and feel deeply about will sooner or later be in our experience.

This Law is like the soil; it doesn't care what kind of seeds we plant; it will produce what is planted. If we plant corn, it won't produce tomatoes. It will grow after its own kind. Likewise, whatever we imagine in our mind, that is what will manifest in our lives.

Misusing the Law can be devastating. It's like using fire to cook or to burn down a house. Or using water to bathe or drown. Or flipping a switch to use electricity to turn on the light or to electrocute someone. Fire, water, or electricity are not good or bad, the use or misuse is just in the way we use them.

When we train the imaging faculty to imagine only good, in a constructive way, it brings into our lives every satisfaction of our desire. Understanding the working of the mental law gives you the control to create.

What If Negative Thoughts Pop Up?

When you want to imagine and create something positive in your life and you receive a negative thought in the process, gently steer your focus in a positive way. Don't turn abruptly with a bang, but focus gently in a different way. When you try with force and effort, things go in a negative direction. Just shew it away like you shew a fly.

The ideal way to get rid of negative emotion is to substitute it or replace it with a positive one. When negative thoughts come into your mind, do not fight them. Mentally replace them with positive or constructive emotions; you replace them with the pleasure of the idea.

Gently turn your mind to the positive with happy memories such as fun times you had with your family or friends. Or think of funny moments that happened. Once you've captured those thoughts, stay in that place for a few minutes. When you stay in the feeling for a short moment, it will start to activate the positive vibration that will cause a new point of attraction in the desired direction. And you will discover that negative thoughts disappear, just like the light dispels the darkness.

It might be that even when you have tried all you can to change the subject in your mind, you still have that same negative thought that keeps popping up. In that case, you must take the time to deal with it. You want to reason with yourself. You may ask yourself:

"Why is this thought making me feel uneasy?"

Now you say, "That was the belief I had before. I didn't know that my thought towards it was the reason I attracted it. I didn't realize that my thinking and feeling created my experience. I didn't know that I was in control of my reality. Now I understand it. From this day forward I will not accept it anymore. I am now releasing all old thoughts and beliefs, and they have all dissipated."

This is an effective way of dissolving old beliefs and stopping the unwanted attraction. If any negative thought surfaces, just take the time to deal with it in that way. Eventually it will fade away.

Your body is a shadow of the mind because when you change your mind, you change your body.

—Unknown

Changing Paths

If a person is always thinking negatively, they have created grooves in that path because it is the one they mentally walk on all the time. Given this habitual thought, it will take practice for them to get on a positive path and start walking there. Because if you walk the same route all the time (that negative path), you'll be so used to it that you walk it unconsciously.

But now that you realize how the Law works, that whatever you focus on you magnify and grow and manifest over time, you might say, "Oh, I've been doing this all wrong. If I am going to create positivity, I am going to have to focus on positive emotions." You have to catch yourself and pay attention to what you are thinking and feeling.

It takes that repetitive practice to create the habitual positive mode. It doesn't just happen in a snap. It takes training the mind into thinking in a new way and into a new, good habit. Then you will know what to do when a negative emotion comes: gently turn it around the other way onto the positive path. It will be easier to do now that you have practiced walking the positive path. Become aware of what you're thinking and feeling. Bring your attention back to the inner world and remind yourself that you want to stay on the positive path.

Understanding the Universal Law is so important! If a person is unaware of it, they won't know how to focus their thoughts and emotions. They will just assume that everything in their life happens by chance or by luck or by accident or by fate. They're ignorant of this truth. But, if they understand this principle, they know that the way they are thinking and feeling creates their destiny and decides their experience. Consequently, they can no longer blame anyone else for their misery or failure. Each and every person creates their own hell and their own heaven by the way they think all day long.

Staying Intentional

I have been asked how to respond to someone who asks about your health before your healing has fully manifested. To reply to a person or a friend who asks that, just say, "My body is on its way to feeling better." Don't allow their question to make you feel a negative emotion about your healing.

As for me, I know I have an Inner Being—Infinite Intelligence—and because my consciousness is taught that way, I'm guiding myself and my body to health. Our bodies are guided by our minds, and they do what our minds tell them to do. And knowing that, I have total freedom.

When you are wanting to become healthy, or prosperous, or successful, you set your intention on that desire. Turn your *attention* to health, wellness, and success. You want to look where you're going.

Similarly, when you're driving down the road, you want to look where you're going, not where you are, and not where you've been. Look in the direction where you're going. Feel the joy of heading towards your destination.

Using the same analogy, when you look where you're going, rather than talking about where you are (current condition), the resistance fades away, and you begin moving in the desired direction.

Don't fall into the trap where a person asks you about your health and you look at the manifested condition, which was the result of previous thoughts that can be released.

Do not be swayed by opinions and negative suggestions of others. When you take control of your mind, negative suggestions of other people have no effect on you.

When you focus your attention on well-being (without fear or worry) and feel the essence of wellness, that feeling *draws* good health to you. Your body has the ability to heal itself. When you're directing your thought, your body follows your thought to its healing.

Here is something important to remember, though: Don't keep checking in with your body, asking, "How's it feeling? How's it feeling?" If you are checking on your healing because you don't yet see the result, you are focusing on what is manifested. You are doubting, and worrying, and not trusting in the process. You're not allowing the Universe to do its work. It's like planting a seed and constantly digging it up to see if it's growing. You're killing it before it has a chance to take root. The soil knows what to do with the seed. Likewise, the creative intelligence that receives our thought and belief objectifies it. Know that the seed has a gestation period, and so will your objective. Allow it to do its work without your constant interruption.

All Healing Is Possible, No Matter the Size

When you get a paper cut, do you get fearful and fret about it and feel it will never heal and believe you will have that paper cut forever? Not usually. You might say, "Ouch, I got a paper cut. That's okay, I'll just wrap it up in a bandage so it's protected, and it'll be gone in a day or two." Right?

It's a small injury; it's just a paper cut. You expect and believe your body will heal that in short order. But when you manifest something big, you don't give your body the same credit for healing. You mentally think, *Oh, wow, that's big. My body can't handle that.*

Your body just healed that paper cut by itself. You didn't have to do anything. You didn't try to force it to be healed. It just knew what to do. The same is true with the "big" stuff. It is how you conceptualize it. When it is simple, you say, "No big deal." When you perceive it as a big thing, you drop into fear and act as if it is not possible to heal from within. It is all a matter of belief.

This is how beliefs create our lives. And it's the same thing with any illness. It's not big or small; the body just heals itself. If a person goes to the doctor and sees an X-ray or CT scan result, they immediately drop into fear, and that fear takes over. If they didn't see that scan or know about it, the body would just heal itself without interruption from them. It would just disappear (as long as they have shifted their thoughts and emotions from the negative that manifested it). But because they saw it, they got afraid. Fear has killed so many people.

Fear makes a disease bigger. If someone didn't look at that manifested condition or they didn't know about it, and they felt good and positive more of the time, the condition would go away and heal itself on its own. (Or your doctor would provide a solution that helps in the healing.) You do have to be strong to not be scared by the current test results, or X-ray, or diagnosis of the doctors. It takes mental toughness to not look at that present condition. But if you can shift your focus to your body, just like with a paper cut that can heal on its own, and you can choose to feel happy and joyful more of the time, it will heal itself. Choose not to allow the disease to grow by feeding into the fear and the chatter all around you. Remember the power of your mind, and you can cancel the chatter and release the fear so your body can do what it needs to do without anything getting in its way.

Protect the environment around you and surround yourself only with positive people. Stay away from the naysayers and others who constantly talk about the gloomy condition. Remember, it is your past thoughts and beliefs that have led to this point. Now creates the future. "The power is in the present moment," says Louise Hay. Things can change from this moment forward. When your doctor makes recommendations, assuming you have turned it over to your Higher Power or Infinite Intelligence, it will be divinely guided for your highest good. Receive your healing however it comes. Allow the Universe to guide the doctors in doing what is best for you. It is the God within you who helps them to help you so you can feel at ease.

These same principles apply to other aspects of life beyond just healing. Money can't buy health, but if you have a rich mind, you can have a rich body, and a rich life.

Tips and Actions

1. Emotion follows thought. Thoughts cause emotion, which will cause whatever you think about to create. Therefore,

do not be concerned about negative situations. Do not be disturbed about unpleasantness. Instead, use the law of substitution. Put positive thoughts in place of negative thoughts. Just replace the thought instead of trying to resist it. No matter what undesirable situation you are in you can always change it. Visualize what you want, like desirable health; change your thinking and the way you feel, and when you think of pleasant thoughts, then the negative thoughts disappear.

2. I use this approach in my own life and see the results and confirmation. The more you use it, the more belief you will have in your ability to shift the negative to a positive. You let go of fear because, if something goes awry, you just replace it with something positive. You will build confidence by practicing it.

3. If you think a thought and it feels bad, you are heading to a negative situation. If you're thinking a thought that feels good, you're attracting positivity into your life. Your emotions tell where you are headed; that's your GPS.

4. Imagine yourself healthy now, doing the activities you enjoy doing. Then your Subjective Mind will respond to your imagery and emotion and the healing takes place.

PART IV

JOURNEY TO HEALING

When you know that negative thinking manifests in
your body, but that your body can heal from within,
you can direct your thoughts and stop the poison
from growing within you.

I had a swollen face, feet, hands, and legs, but I was still working. I wasn't really me. I couldn't concentrate. I couldn't focus. It was just my body drifting places. I had shortness of breath, an intense cough, diarrhea, and bloody stools. My family and I were on a two-hour drive home from a meeting when things took a serious turn.

We stopped at a rest area, and my daughter and I went to the bathroom. She heard a gushing sound and asked what that was. I looked and to my surprise, I saw blood squirting out.

I paused and didn't answer her for a short while. Finally I told her that it was all blood. She began to look up the symptoms online. She started trembling and crying. I looked at her and almost yelled at her saying, "I am fine. I am fine." She said my face was so pale. She kept asking if I wanted water. I told her no.

As we were walking back to the cars, my husband walked along with my son, but didn't know what had happened in the restroom. I hadn't told him yet. We were all driving there in two vehicles and my daughter was riding with her brother. My husband and I were in the other car.

When my daughter told her brother what she saw me experience in the bathroom, my son was in shock. As we were pulling out of the parking lot, he was gesturing with his hands to get our attention. As my husband drove out, my son then called me on my cell phone, and asked me if I had full coverage insurance. I put him on speaker phone and said, yes. He proceeds to tell my husband, his dad, to drive me straight to the emergency room.

I said, I wanted to go home first and that I would make an appointment tomorrow. I told him it was not an emergency. But in reality, it was not doable in the morning because it would've been Sunday and they were not open for regular hours. But I wanted to go home first because I had not been home all day already. He kept insisting that his dad drive me straight to the emergency room.

At the Emergency Room

It was already eight o'clock in the evening on a Saturday, so when we arrived, most of the doors were locked. When I got out of the car to enter the hospital, I could barely walk even ten steps before I was out of breath. I couldn't breathe. When I finally found a door to enter, I was registered and was taken to a room to be checked out. While there, the emergency doctor did a COVID test. This was the start of the pandemic—March 14, 2020.

They ran other tests too. They didn't find any COVID, but my blood level was very low. The doctor kept telling me, repeatedly, that my blood was very low. He probably didn't think I knew the meaning, but I didn't think anything of it.

Then another doctor came in the room, a female doctor, and she also said my blood level was very low. At the time, I didn't understand the gravity of it. So she said, "let me draw a picture." She explained that normal blood level ranges from a low of seven and to normal being fourteen. And mine was a three.

I happened to be on the phone with my husband and the kids because they were not allowed to come back into the exam room with me. They could hear what the doctors were explaining to me.

The doctor said, "We have to give you a blood transfusion."

I said, "Today?" I was hesitant because I've never had this before and I didn't want anybody's blood. I asked them if there was any other way, because I wanted to be safe. They didn't really respond. They knew they had to save me with the blood transfusion. It turned out I needed four units of blood to get up to a seven, which was acceptable.

The Diagnosis

My husband spent the night in the hospital with me. The next day, the doctor told me and my husband that I was like the walking dead because nobody walked at a blood level three. The lowest he'd seen was a five. They had also run more tests and found I had RSV (respiratory syncytial virus), which is a respiratory infection, and they also did a CT scan, a colonoscopy, and a test on my uterus.

The colonoscopy showed cancer, I call it C of the colon. One of the ICU doctors informed me what she saw, and she was very concerned. She wanted to keep pointing out that it was C and she kept repeating it. They kept saying they were very concerned. I looked at her while she was saying it and I was still. I was very quiet as she was explaining; I stayed very still, very quiet, and very calm. I didn't say anything to her. And then she asked me, "Do you understand what I'm saying?"

I said to her, "Why do you keep repeating it? Because you want me to be hysterical? You want me to be terrified? But because I'm calm, you think that I don't understand you?"

She said, "Yes. Why are you so calm?"

When she was telling me the diagnosis with that C, I did not accept it in my mind. My mind just blocked it out. I claimed God to be my healer, that Infinite Intelligence is healing me. I have the healing Presence within me that is healing me. After claiming that, I felt a sense of security. I felt safe.

Now a few days had passed. One surgeon came into my room and was going to schedule surgery, but because of the RSV, said it wasn't safe to do it until it cleared up first. So they treated the respiratory infection first.

Then the colorectal surgeon told me to stick around and not go home because he was trying to schedule my surgery in a few days. If I went home, it would be hard to schedule and get me back in to get the surgery because of all the COVID-19 patients. This is already after more than a week in the hospital. The results from the test he had done hadn't come back yet to confirm, but because he felt he knew what it was, he wanted to schedule the surgery.

He said, "I'm going to try to push to get the results in early. Normally it takes two or three days, but I'm going try to push it to get them early."

I felt he was my guidance, my protector. He was looking out for me. I didn't know this doctor, but because I called for protection, everything was lined up for me. I felt so cared for. They could have released me, but he said stay around for two more days.

The Recommendation: Surgery

After ten days in the hospital, my doctor came in and told me that he had all the arrangements made: the surgeon along with other staff. So the morning before surgery, I had to sign a consent form. The doctors explained the process to me and that it was major surgery and that the machine would do the breathing for me during that time. My mind was wondering if I would wake up from being asleep or not. Would I survive the surgery or not, given that it was so critical that a machine is breathing for me? *Shake off that thought.*

My family was not allowed to be with me when I signed the consent form because it was the beginning of COVID-19 in 2020.

During all of that, I was actually alone. The doctor said that this surgery is not a guarantee and that some people need multiple surgeries to get through this. At this point, I gathered all my thoughts together, thinking of all the wisdom I have learned, and started using the process in my mind.

I said, "God arranged the right doctors for me and all the right staff. God directs the doctor to do all the right things and guides me and guides all others to do what is right for me. I am protected and being cared for, and all is well." I was strong. I canceled out what was pronounced to me. I just thought of God, the *power greater than all.*

After thinking all these prayers, I felt a sense of ease and security. I felt protected. I felt trusting. I felt safe as if I were a child and I was well taken care of and protected. I also imagined being at home and doing the things I would normally do when I was well. I was in the kitchen having fun with my family and doing my cooking that I normally would do. My husband even had video calls with me where he went through our home so I could see and feel how great it was to be back home. It was such a natural feeling. I felt the joy of being in my home. I was well in my imagination. I felt vital and strong with a sense of happiness and wellness.

But while I was imagining being home, my family was at home without me. My husband later told me how he went home from the hospital before my surgery feeling a sense of loss. When he walked into the house, he felt its emptiness without me. He was used to me being everywhere, but now all the rooms were empty. He looked at the cultural dresses that I wear for my performances and wondered,

What will I do with all these dresses! (They cost several hundred dollars each.) He didn't know what to think or feel. He was going through more than I knew.

My children and husband all feared that my diagnosis was fatal. Each of them had to handle their feelings on their own, because they could not see me during this time. Without them visiting me, it just made it worse. I could not show them my strength and resolve.

I was awakened probably four hours after surgery in the recovery room. I was being monitored after surgery. I was not able to open my eyes or make any other bodily movements yet; I was still out of it from the deep sleep. I remembered I was supposed to call my family. My husband was home awaiting my phone call and starting to panic. The nurse who monitored me said that the doctor had notified my husband already about being out of surgery, but I knew they were still awaiting my personal call. When the nurses brought me back to my room, I was able to text him. I wasn't able to talk until a few hours later. I realized I went through major surgery safely. The doctors kept me there three days afterwards.

It's a miracle because I got through the medical crisis with the one surgery, and it was perfect and right. I prayed for it. I asked for it. I claimed it. So getting my mind right in the beginning, before the process started, allowed for perfection. Mind work aligned all things into place. And everyone that was involved with me was in the right place taking the right action. The mind is powerful.

Steps to Recovery

I was released from the hospital after fourteen days. I was sent home with some pain medication and iron pills to take. And then I was scheduled to do chemotherapy for six months. The doctor assigned to do the chemo consulted with me and asked if I would prefer to start soon or to wait until COVID-19 is over. It was still early in the COVID-19 pandemic. She said that the immune system would be low from chemo, and they wanted it to be safe for me. The doctor suggested that it's more effective to get it done right away. So, I agreed to start right away in spite of the intensity of COVID-19.

Again, at this point, I felt I would be protected even with the low immunity from the treatment. I felt it would be safe for me when I went to get my port implanted in my chest under the skin. (This port would stay under my skin throughout treatment and make it easier to receive intravenous fluids or chemotherapy medications each time I received treatment.)

A week later, I had my first chemotherapy treatment. Then for six months, during that time, I had regular doctor visits with the hematologist, which is the chemo doctor. I had monthly visits with her to keep up with the progress. During that time, I had some numbness in my hands, fingers, and feet due to the side effects of the drugs.

After chemo, I had another colonoscopy. That was exactly a year after the first one. They did a CT scan every six months. And when the test came back, they said it was all clear. The results said it was all perfect. The oncology doctor called after six months of the completion of treatment to check in and ask how about the numbness in my hands, fingers, and feet. I said no, I don't have any more numbness. I felt like myself again, completely normal and well. The blood work that she ran regularly was normal, the colonoscopy was normal, and the CT scan was normal. Up to this writing, all is fine and all is perfect.

I recovered and healed and completed my treatment during the same time period as when the restrictions from the pandemic were lifted. I now have functions and parties regularly because I sing at events. But, because this all happened during the pandemic, nobody knew about my journey, as if the whole thing never happened. The timing was perfect. All that I mentally pictured came to pass.

Hindsight

For the two years prior to my diagnosis, I was not aware that I had lost a lot of weight. I said to my husband, "I need to get all my pants fixed, the ones with elastic waistband; they are all too loose." I didn't know that the loose clothes were from the drastic weight loss. I lost at least half of my body weight. A lot of friends asked me what my weight loss secret was. Eventually they started saying I should stop losing weight because I was losing too much. And in my mind, I thought, *I kinda like being nice and thin, and I'm not even trying to lose weight*, but I didn't tell them that. Then after being in the hospital for two weeks, and being put on a liquid diet, I left the hospital looking like skin and bones. I looked like a corpse. My husband was concerned. He tried nourishing me. He cooked what he could, but because I had never let him in the kitchen, all he knew how to make was BBQ. He made a lot of it during that time! He also went to buy donuts every morning to help me gain my weight back.

Now I have gained back all my weight and then some. I am so healthy now. I had my family there as my supporters; they helped throughout. My daughter drove me to chemo every week. I am fortunate to have my family.

I have said before that nothing happens by chance. When I reflect back on the blood transfusion I had at the hospital, the four units of blood that I needed, I know I am divinely guided. The nurse giving me my transfusions punctured one of the units of blood I was about to receive. She poked a hole in it and there was blood spilled everywhere. She tried to tape it, but wasn't successful. They had to discard it and replace it with a new one.

When I returned home, and reflected on that, I knew why it happened. I believe that one packet was not the right one for me or something might be wrong with it. I had asked for guidance and protection, and my protector, my Inner Being, caused her to make that mistake; it caused a break in that bag. It had to be discarded. Understand the Law; nothing just happens by chance. I asked for protection, and if it was not the right one for me, it caused her to discard it.

Divine Timing

At the hospital, the time of my surgery was delayed because the doctor and staff had meetings due to new COVID-19 protocols. My original surgery schedule was to be in the afternoon, but it was pushed to the next morning. They said I would be the first person on the doctor's schedule for surgery at eight o'clock in the morning. When they pushed it back, I felt a sense of relief because it gave me more time to work on myself, more time to get my own assurance and feel completely secured. If it had still been scheduled for the regular time that afternoon, I wouldn't have been ready mentally. My mind would not have been prepped yet. And the doctor would not have been as fresh and ready for my surgery. I'm glad it was pushed back.

In addition to the timing of the surgery itself, it was divine timing for me to get into the hospital before the total COVID-19 shutdown. As it was, my family could only come in one at a time at first, then not at all. I had to go through much of that alone. But if I had not been admitted to the hospital at that time, they may have had to postpone surgery until after the pandemic wave. And how much more blood would I have lost? Would I have been able to survive?

Even a few months later, they may not have even said I could come into the hospital or even come in to get chemo. They could have said, "We can't even schedule your surgery because we have all these people dying of COVID-19." If the timing wasn't perfect … I might not have beat all of that. In order for the doctors who were supposed to be a part of my healing to play a role, the timing had to be right.

It gives me chills to think that a way was being made for me to be taken care of like I'm God's child. As if God said, "This is my child; you take care of my child's schedule. Get her this time, that time…." It was like the road was paved for me to get that done.

Miraculous Results

When I returned home from the hospital, my regular doctor, whom I had not seen for many years, called me on a Sunday to say she was looking at my health records and test results. She said everything looked so healthy that she couldn't believe I was in a hospital, went through surgery, and went through all those conditions.

Everyone was amazed I had recovered so fast. The doctors had never seen anyone in their career have a blood level of three, and survive, and live to tell the story. My doctor said I had an incredible story to tell. A week later, my doctor said, "You should teach people. They want to hear from those who recovered rather than from a doctor." I was honored when she said that. But I was also well cared for: from Infinite Intelligence to the team of eight nurses, surgeons, and staff in that operating room. Throughout the whole time in the hospital, from beginning to end, despite my journey, I had such a wonderful, awesome, pleasant experience with all the hospital staff, doctors, and nurses. It could not have been any better. I was well cared for like a queen.

A few days after coming home, I learned of at least three other people who had the same C diagnosis. Two of them died, and one of them went through four rounds of chemotherapy that constantly drained him. My husband told me that I was nothing like that. Everybody may have a different experience because everybody feels differently and offers a feeling or releases their feelings differently to the Universe. Because I don't talk about it, they don't know. They just think, *Oh, you're so different than all those people.*

When you're done with chemo, they run tests again (a colonoscopy and CT) to make sure all is clear before removing the chemo/IV port. The day I went in, there were two or three nurses there talking amongst themselves. They were saying, "It doesn't look like she was a chemo patient. Look at her full head of hair."

I'm just so thankful. My hair was thinning, but through it all, I still had a head of hair. I had a number three blood level, I seemed like the walking dead, and now I am healed. I am just in awe. I am very thankful. I'm protected. This is what using the mind constructively does—it heals.

Serendipity

My son Brandon was my savior through this. Oh my God. My son's the one who got me into the hospital. He's the one who saved me. Literally. He said, "Mom, you need to go. Dad, you need to drive her straight to the hospital." He was so insistent.

A little side story is that Brandon's birthday is August 1. Well, when they gave me the blood transfusion, they could only give me up to seven units total (four more than I had). And then the heart will pump on its own to raise blood to a sufficient level. Before surgery, my blood levels kept dropping because I kept bleeding, but then after surgery and everything, the blood level stayed at 8.1 for the four days until I checked out from the hospital. It didn't dawn on me until I was home and my daughter said, "Mom, you know, Brandon's birthday is August 1 (8/1)." That gave me chills!

Even more interesting is when I was leaving the hospital. I was being wheeled out by a nurse who was twenty-six years old, just like my son. But guess what his name was? His name was Brandon. How could that be? My son's the one who got me into the hospital. And another Brandon wheeled me out of it. And they were the same age! Wow. I didn't realize all of that until my daughter pointed out.

How Did I Even Attract This?

I have been asked, "How did you attract this? Nothing just happens by chance. So how did you attract all this?"

I didn't understand it in the beginning.

And then as I dug deeper, I knew how it happened. There's a cause behind it that had been brewing for at least two years. You see, I was always in a hurry to get to work. I was always rushing because I didn't allow enough time to drive to work. I stayed up late spending so much time cooking and cleaning the kitchen, packing my husband's lunch every night, which I have done since we were first married. And by the time I would shower and go to bed, it was around 3:00 AM and I had to be at work in the morning. So I didn't get enough sleep.

Then I was always rushing to get ready for work and driving there. I did discover later on that my *hurry* was Fear. After a long period of time, it does run the body down. It poisons the cells in the body and causes disease. My body and mind were in so much tension, strain, and stress most of the time that I wasn't aware of it, and for a long period of time. All those tensions caused it to break down. And that was the cause of my illness.

At first, I refused to see all that weight loss and what was going on with my body. I refused to go to the doctor, despite the urging from my family and my clients. I was trying to pretend to do the normal things, but I was so thin and out of energy. Still I refused to admit anything was wrong.

I said, "I'm not going to a doctor. I don't want to hear what they have to tell me."

But then when the blood started flowing and it all came to a head, that's when I said, "Okay, I'm going to allow the doctor to do what they need to do." But at the same time, I know God is within me to help me and to guide them. I gave that permission. I decided that what they proposed felt in line with my Inner Being. Along with God, within me, helping them see, I can let go. And when I felt that security, I released. I relieved that tension because I knew they were going help me. And most importantly, like I said, God is within me helping me and guiding them to do the right work. It was a feeling of security. And I felt at ease. I felt at peace with what they were doing.

But now I know how to think differently and change things in the future. The important thing is that I discovered why and how it happened. There's nothing to fear, because I know I'm in control of anything in my experience. That is my power.

The Story of a Little Pill

One evening before the C diagnosis I had taken a pain pill. It was Norco, a prescription from the doctor. On New Year's Eve, I wanted to ring in the new year, in a welcoming way, an appropriate way, I believed. I poured a little champagne, not even half of the glass but a few sips worth, to toast in with my husband. In my mind I thought, *I'm not supposed to mix pain medicine with alcohol,* but I also thought, *It has already been a couple of hours, maybe it has already worn off.* That was my intuition nudging me in the first thought, you see? But I opposed it with the second thought. It's not like I didn't have a warning.

Within the next few hours, I went to take a shower and I felt like I was about to pass out. I wasn't able to stand. I felt lifeless. It was kind of hard to describe, but it was as if I couldn't breathe, and as if I wasn't living at the same time. I realized it was that mixing of the two substances. I had this feeling that I wouldn't be able to hang on or make it through, as I remembered what I had learned from one of the past teachers.

He said there was a man who took poison by mistake. He was a hundred miles from the nearest hospital and had no way of getting there on time. He was a student of the laws of mind. He used his mind power and called on the Infinite Presence, God. He called to God to neutralize the poison substance in his body. And within a short time he felt relief.

I remembered that and I used that same principle. I said, "God, Infinite Intelligence, which dwells within me, neutralize this toxin from my body. I am claiming this healing Presence within me and to free me now. I give thanks."

And I was able to get through with my shower. I was still a little weak in the morning. But the next morning I was fine, and the next day was fine. I later learned that my son's friend's mom passed away from that same type of incident, and I was shocked. When I realized how understanding the wisdom and the knowledge of Laws and applying them with confidence and belief saves you.

I talked myself out of paying attention. Had I listened to intuition, I wouldn't have gone through that. We always have this guidance within us, this intuition. Some call it instinct in animals. We have to be aware of and pay attention to that small voice from within. It's how we live through life successfully.

This happened at the beginning of 2020, before the C diagnosis. And because I learned this new year lesson on listening to intuition first, I knew how to use the power of mind with my later C diagnosis.

What I Now Know

All illness starts with negative emotion. It first takes place in the mind. And permanent healing must also take place in the mind. By directing our thoughts to thinking harmoniously, in turn we'll have healthy bodies.

It doesn't matter the size of the illness, big or small, early stage or full blown; you don't resist it, you don't fight against it. Instead make peace with it. Just say, "It is what it is." Then find better feeling thought; not all at once, but gently and gradually. Your guidance system is letting you know which way you're feeling. When you've reached that better feeling thought, then you're making a shift in your vibration. It's all about energy flow. Once you've gotten control of the way you feel, now you're in power. When you know the cause is vibrational, its origin is entirely mental, you now know how to turn it around by replacing the thought, by aligning with your higher self. Then you can say, "It's no big deal, I'm not afraid of this." Nothing should be a concern; nothing is a problem. With that knowledge, life is no longer a challenge, but rather it's an opportunity for expansion.

Tips and Actions

1. Recognize that nothing happens by chance. Whatever has manifested in your life was created by past thoughts, feelings, and actions.

2. That means you have the power to shift your current results by changing your thoughts and feelings in the direction you want to go.

3. Free your mind and body from strain, stress, and tension by paying attention to the way you feel and catching the negative feeling in the early, subtle stage—and by using your mind to direct your thought to feeling good more of the time.

4. Follow your guidance—that inner small voice within you. It could save you from making a faulty decision.

PART V

THREE STEPS TO HEALING

"You have the power to heal your life, and you need to know that. We think so often that we are helpless, but we're not. We always have the power of our minds... claim and consciously use your power."

–Louise L. Hay

God or Infinite Intelligence is the only power. When we call on the Presence within, it saturates our minds and bodies, and we receive it to make us whole. Then we begin to function harmoniously.

In reality, the human body is really perfect. But it's covered up with wrong thinking. We came into this world with a perfect body no matter how a person appears. All we do is uncover the perfection that is within us already. That is what healing is. Uncovering, neutralizing, and erasing images of thought and letting perfections come through.

When a person realizes that everything operates through the mind, and the instrument of healing is thought, then you see that nothing can permanently heal without right thinking.

Diseases and limitations are simply images of thought, and thought will evaporate when you turn away from it. It only receives the nourishment when you give it your attention.

There are no incurable diseases. Realize that you are working with the Infinite Intelligence that made your body, and that this healing Presence is available at all times. You have access to this creative power that operates through your own mind to bring anything you desire into your life.

One of the teachers from the past, Joseph Murphy, stated that an engraving found written over an ancient temple reads, "The doctor dresses the wound, and God heals the patient." A surgeon removing a tumor is removing a block to make way for the healing of God to flow through. Likewise, a psychologist or psychiatrist gets rid of mental blocks, then advises the patient to take on a new way of thinking, which will then allow a pathway for harmony.

We can believe that a cut will heal itself, but we have a harder time believing in healing for something bigger. And belief is what drives the healing. When it is a little thing like a bruise or scraped knee, we think we can heal it. It is the same with money; manifesting $10 or $10,000 is the same thing. Size or amount does not matter; it is only where the *intention* is directed upon.

The Three Steps to Healing

How you apply these three steps, as you will learn more about in this chapter, will determine your success in healing.

First step:

Remain calm and do not be afraid of the manifested condition.

Second step:

Realize that the condition is only the result of past thinking and belief, which have no more effect on you.

Third step:

Mentally claim the mighty healing power of God that is within you.

This process will end all mental toxins from growing.

When you have been diagnosed with an illness, do not be frightened. Realize that the manifestation is only an indication of your past vibration. It's letting you know how you've been thinking. It's not the big concern that people make it out to be. Present manifestation is just an indication of your past thinking. You don't have to accept it, and you don't have to remain there. Just offer a current new vibration, and when the vibration changes, then everything must change in response to your "now" frequency. You have the ability to change your outcome, because you have control over your emotion and your thought. You have a guidance system that lets you know which way you're thinking and feeling. With this knowledge comes empowerment. Do not be swayed by others' opinions and fears. Use the God-given power to create the life you deserve and desire.

Fear Perpetuates Disease

When the doctor gives a diagnosis, most people get frightened by that pronouncement. They accept it, they feel trapped, and they assume they don't have a way out. The fear of hearing that diagnosis takes over their body so fast. Abraham-Hicks says that fear of dying or death, is what kills more than the disease itself. The minute someone is diagnosed, they get into a panic mode; they feel powerless.

It takes a strong being to cancel out that fear, but when you have the knowledge and understanding of the Laws of Mind, you are not too concerned by the news. You can remain calm knowing that you have Divine power to neutralize it. You rise in consciousness to overcome that fear and take control over the situation. You refocus, get aligned with your higher self, and then move into wholeness.

Turn Away from the Manifested Condition

This is worth mentioning many times on this subject matter, because it is of great importance.

If your current condition is not what you want, then detach your attention from it. You must think a different thought. You can't look at the appearance of things without attracting more of it. It's the way Laws of the Universe work.

Replace the unwanted thoughts with the thoughts you do want, thoughts that feel GOOD to you. Keep in mind not to use effort, because effort is forcing, which will cause resistance. Instead, feel it with EASE and a relaxed, good feeling state of mind.

To think is to create. Use right thinking to imagine and visualize and feel in your mind your ideal health or desires. Feel the naturalness of it, and you will objectify it into your reality.

Now Your Doctor Can Get to Work

If you're getting a procedure done, or before doing any activity, it is best to set an intention for the way you want it to go. Then, the Universe paves the path for you and delivers that intent to you.

I will give an illustration: The day prior to my surgery, I was preparing my mind for a successful outcome. I said to myself, "Infinite Spirit within me is my healing agent, and all is well." Afterwards, I felt at ease, the feeling of comfort, and certainty, and I felt protected. I was feeling as if it's *already* a successful surgery. I stated it in a way that it's already done, and in the right way, even though the whole thing is about to take place. The point is to present to the Universe your *desired* outcome, and the intention *must* match the outcome. It is Law. The outside mirrors the inside.

I used the power of my mind to get in alignment. Once I did the vibrational work—the mental work—all the worries, concerns, and fears were lifted. I felt the assurance of a desired outcome; I had a feeling of an accomplished fact.

After the mental work is done, when it comes time for surgery, whatever the surgeon does is a success, a wonderful outcome. This mental process also drew to me the most amazing, knowledgeable doctor. I am thankful for the marvelous result.

On the other hand, if a person is ignorant of the Laws of Mind, they might be feeling afraid, worried, or uneasy, thinking that something might go wrong or that the surgery might not be a success. If they're thinking in that way, then they will not get a good result from it. It is *not* that they don't have the right surgeon. Some may secretly blame the doctor. But it's their own attraction, according to their thinking. That's using the Laws of Mind in the wrong way. It's as though they are shooting themselves in the foot. The Universe will give them the experience to match that feeling. It is returning to them the condition of how they're vibrating, what they're emitting, negatively or positively.

This is why having the knowledge, the understanding, and the right application of the Laws of the Universe is of great value.

The power is in your own consciousness—your mind.
It is the use of consciousness that brings it into your
life—through your thoughts, feelings, and beliefs.

—Chantha Pak

I personally have no objection to any form of healing. Anything that will help us to relieve pain and suffering is good, whether it is a pill or surgery. And I gratefully acknowledge the wonderful work of doctors and medical practitioners and the work that they have done and continue to do. I have no controversy with anyone on the subject of healing. I am happy when anyone is healed or helped by any method. Any and all methods of healing must be good.

The life and reality of people are spiritual and mental, and until negative thoughts are healed, no form of cure will be permanent. Those who have knowledge of this silent power of mind are putting it to use to heal their bodies and bring success into their lives.

This mental Law is always working in accordance with our belief. Beliefs are powerful. You get what you believe, because the Universe is supporting that belief; not because of a cosmic truth, but because someone held it as their vibrational awareness. Belief makes things happen.

The Power of Suggestion and Source

Joseph Murphy's book, *The Power of Your Subconscious Mind,* talks about how to use a placebo. They had two groups of cancer patients who were given a placebo for treatment. One group was told by the doctor that they were given the medication to heal them. The other group was given the same placebo pill and message that it would cure their cancer, but from a nurse, not a doctor. Seventy percent of those who were given the placebo by the doctor were healed, but only twenty percent of those told by the nurse were healed.

The doctors concluded that the healing came from their belief. The two groups had the same illness and were given the same placebo, but one group believed, "Oh, the doctor gave me this. I am taking it and I am cured." Their belief cured them. The other group did not have a strong belief because it came from a nurse, so only twenty percent were cured. It all leads to belief.

"Man is belief expressed."

—Phineas Quimby

In my case, I had only one surgery. I am so blessed. Others with the same cancer have had multiple surgeries, and some did not survive. My belief was that I'm cared for and protected by my Higher Power, that Higher Power is God, who guided the doctors to do the right thing the first time. Other people were worried or fearful and it took several times in and out of surgery to reach their result.

"With every pill we have prescribed for us we should also be given a creative prayer, a suggested way to correct our destructive patterns of thought."

—Ernest Holmes

Decide How You Want to Feel

Make the decision on how you want your body to feel; don't let it come through mass consciousness. Don't let others affect how you feel.

When I received the first vaccine shot for COVID-19 in May of 2020, I had a sore arm. When it was time for the second one

(Pfizer®), I thought in my mind, *My body now knows this drug, so my body won't react to it; my body is strong.* I said to it, "There will be no soreness."

While at the vaccine center, I curiously asked the nurse, "Is the second one going to hurt?"

She said, "You will have the same soreness." She had a pamphlet, but I didn't want to read it because I didn't want to put that information into my mind.

If I was not mindful, my mind would have been open to receive what is mentioned in that pamphlet. I guarded my mind against that information and had no soreness at all. I was almost not sure I even had the shot! I didn't even feel where the needle was until I touched the spot. I heard of other people feeling sick, but I barely felt a prick. My daughter said I should be the role model so the world will not feel anything. I made up my mind not to feel anything.

Decide to override the belief of mass consciousness regarding an issue. Your body follows your mind. I was evidence of that. My body responded to me.

When you believe something, it will become real, whether you stay focused on it or not. It all starts with the emotion, the feeling.

If you are not aware, negativity and false suggestions can seep into your mind. When people watch the news on TV, they often leave their mind open to all kinds of suggestions, not having an intention of what *not* to accept. Commercials on TV encourage people to fight *against,* which only creates more of the things they don't want, because the *attention* is on what they are fighting against. "What you resist, persists." Others don't realize it, but the information slips in slowly and they are open to their negative suggestions. Make a conscious choice of what you let into your mind.

"Energy flows where attention goes," is another phrase used in quantum physics. If you focus your attention on something, it intensifies and grows. When you focus your attention on fighting against drugs or cancer (or any subject), you bring more energy to it and it expands. Choose where you want your energy to flow.

Choose a Happy, Healthy Life

I once met a woman who truly chose how she wanted to feel and it paid off for her. While I was a hairdresser, a friend of mine referred a woman to me who was 106 years old! I was so excited. I wanted to meet her. I was so thrilled that I got my camera ready the night before to take pictures with her. She had been in the paper as one of the oldest living survivors of the San Francisco earthquake of 1906.

When I finally got to meet her, I was talking to her and was studying her at the same time—observing her. I asked her what her secret was to healthy living. At the time, I was just starting to learn about Universal Laws. I wasn't advanced yet.

So, I asked her the secret to a long, healthy life, and she said she ate everything she wanted, but most of all, she stayed happy. She was very joyful. She shared with me of her childhood, and about her family. She was so focused. I was so shocked of how she remembered everything.

She was so pleasant and charming. I enjoyed her vibe and her energy. And even though she was 106, she looked to me as if she were sixty-five.

She was so full of life and joy. I had so much fun talking to her, and I was so honored to have this one-on-one private time with her for three hours. And now it makes me realize how she fed her mind with joy and happiness, which contributed to her long life. She demonstrated how a healthy mind creates a healthy body. She not only lived a long life, but a long AND healthy life. She lived to be 108 years old. Amazing! She lived alone at her age. Can you believe it?

Treating a Cold and Flu

For years, when I went to work, people around me were always getting sick. They always had colds and they said, "Chantha never gets a cold." And I would tell them the remedies. They then said, "Oh, you should write a book." Well, here is the book and the remedies that have worked for me for years.

When you're feeling exhausted or you feel fatigued or sleepy, that's a first sign of a cold coming on. You recognize it by that and a subtle sore throat. At this point, you can stop the cold before it gets full blown.

Note, though, you are not to accept that it's a cold. Disown it. Usually, a person would say, "Oh my goodness, I'm coming down with a cold." And they mentally accept it, and it grabs hold. Instead say, "I'm not accepting this. Therefore I'm doing these remedies and I know that these remedies will help raise my immune system to fight it off." It may be that someone around you is not feeling well, and you feel uneasy about it, so you do the remedies to build up your body and stop it before it starts.

That reminds me of Abraham-Hicks. When someone asked, "How do you stop a problem?" Her answer was, "Before it starts." She illustrated with this analogy: If you were to put your car on top of a hill and nudge it a little, you are able to stop it. But when it's halfway downhill and you try to stop it; you cannot. The momentum is so strong that it will run you over. Likewise, with this remedy treatment, you can nip it in the bud.

Mentally position yourself. How? The first step is to build up in your mind; understand and know that your cells are *intelligent*. They know what to do; they know how to get rid of intruders. Second, do not accept a cold. This is essential.

Cold Remedies

Below is the physical work, the remedies to help strengthen the body.

1. Gargle with warm salt water (one tablespoon of salt to four-to-six ounces of water) three or four times per day.

2. Rinse nose with distilled salt water. You can cup water in your hand and inhale and flush it out or use a nasal aspirator. The nose and throat are connected, so you can do both. The salt water disinfects your nasal passages and rinses pollen and other impurities away.

3. Chew on fresh garlic. Chew two raw garlic cloves with food. (Chewing them with food will ease the burn, or you may want to chop them up and put them into a soup, but DO NOT cook them. They need to be raw for the potency.)

4. Take echinacea tablets (an herbal supplement) according to the instructions on the bottle (usually two every four hours). Take them right after a meal or with a snack. You can also drink echinacea tea.

In addition to these remedies, get plenty of rest. It is important that a person gets fully rested; get a full night's rest for the body to gain strength. Repeat this consistently for the first few days and until the symptoms clear.

Drink plenty of fluids. It is good to drink carrot juice and cranberry juice (no sugar added). They are powerhouses of antioxidants and vitamins.

So for me, I use the remedies at the first sign of those symptoms, and constantly concentrate on the remedies. Generally, after the second day I feel better, but I keep doing it until all symptoms are completely gone. I also take chewable Vitamin C, drink the juices noted above, and avoid all caffeine during that period. This is an all-natural approach, so I won't need cough medicine or any medications. I have been using these remedies for the past twenty years and they are very effective for me.

You can also use your imagination to breathe out black clouds (impurities) and breathe in bright light (health and healing). Lie down in a comfortable position, then visualize black clouds leaving from your body as you're breathing out and breathe in bright light into your body. Do three to five breaths before falling off to sleep and before getting up in the morning. This is a very effective process for healing.

The flu is more intense than a cold. Its symptoms may be stronger. A cold may seem to give you lead time to prepare to fight it off.

The flu is different.

Once I went to a party and two days later, I felt flu symptoms. It attacked my body strongly and my chest was just pounding. Later that evening before falling off to sleep, I began to work on myself. I got into a relaxed state, knowing that the healing Presence is within me. That night I had a dream, and in my dream, the figure stripped away the flu from my body. Similar to how you would strip a sheet away from the bed. It was surreal. When I awakened, I felt such relief.

Your Path to Permanent Wholeness (Preventing a Relapse)

People might ask, "What if a person had a healing but some months later, they had a relapse to the former condition?"

This happens because after the healing, the person may reinfect himself by accepting a suggestion of fear or by entering into other emotional disturbance, like anger or hate.

People must change their habits of thought and adopt right thinking, right feeling, and right action. The physical illness will be cleared once the inner problem is clear. After learning about disease and illness, they must decide to discontinue the wrong thinking that produced the ill-effect in their life. And after learning all about the disease and illness and what caused the misfortune in their world, their reality, they will then maintain a consciousness of health, peace, and harmony. And they will then prevent a relapse or reinfection of the former destructive emotions so they will then produce permanent healing.

If they keep falling back on the wrong thinking and negative emotion, they may relapse into illness. They have to maintain right thinking. They create their experiences in life from beliefs that they have nurtured. That's what keeps disease there. It is the vibration they are emitting from their consciousness. Every joy, sorrow, success, or failure reflects the belief, thought, and emotion that a person has focused upon in their mind, which they are attracting into their experience.

It is of the greatest importance in decisions. Decide to not let the evidence of the disease of others or whatever unwanted condition that they have created in their life affect you, because it has nothing to do with you. It is their experience which they have attracted with their thoughts. You have control of your own experience, and it is deciding what you want and then directing your thinking in harmony with the Laws of the Universe, believing that your desire is an accomplished fact.

Belief makes thoughts very powerful. I had a realization that the Presence of God is the most powerful healing agency known to the human mind. The Laws of the Universe, which are Laws of Mind, will operate for us to the fullest extent of our belief in and understanding of it. And you need no creed for this Law to work for you. It works regardless of any religion a person may have, or even when they have no religion at all. It works for all alike. A person learns that their Inner Being, which is God within, is the creator of his/her body and also heals it. We have to have that awareness and that belief. Without that understanding, it will not operate accordingly. It operates through us, which is through our state of consciousness. It is what we think, feel, and believe. It is the invisible inner working; it is a silent builder.

Simply know that you are a spiritual being, and the state of Spirit is perfect. Healing is a revelation; for the revealing of the perfect being (from false thought) always heals.

Anyone can heal who believes they can; and that belief comes from knowing that the healing Presence of God is within us. We can contact it with our thoughts.

To daily imagine and to daily declare the perfect image of oneself is the correct mental practice, and it will heal.

Tips and Actions

1. All diseases are curable. Realize that Infinite Intelligence made your body and it can heal it.
2. Allow yourself to feel the comfort and ease of knowing that God is working all things to your good. Bless the medical professionals around you who are in alignment with God's healing power.
3. Thinking is creating. Stay healthy by maintaining right thoughts, feelings, and beliefs.

4. Decide what you want and give your attention only to that, and the Universe will bring it into your reality.

5. This mental law operates according to our belief. Whatever we believe, we draw into our life.

6. The Law gives you the power to overcome your weakness, no matter how often you may have failed in the past.

7. The healing presence of God is within us. We can contact it with our thoughts.

8. Tune in on the Infinite and let the peace and harmony of God flow through you.

DAILY MEDITATIONS FOR HEALING

I believe these meditations will be helpful to all who take the time to use them.

First, decide which meditation you wish to use, then get into a comfortable position. The body should be relaxed, but the mentality should be active. Then read the meditation several times, attempting to realize the meaning of the words, and to enter into the atmosphere of the thought. Meditate upon the words until you feel a sense of realization.

BODILY PERFECTION

The spirit within me is God.
Every part of my body is made of spiritual substance; there is a spiritual body which cannot be sick.

The healing power of God is now flowing through me, healing me, and making me whole.

The Infinite Healing Presence made me. It knows how to heal.

It knows all the processes and functions of my body, and I claim that the Holy Spirit is flowing through me now—animating, healing, and restoring my whole being to wholeness, beauty, and perfection.

The inner power of life within me is God.
Every breath I draw is a breath of perfection, revitalizing, upbuilding, and renewing every cell of my body.

I'm giving thanks for the miraculous healing power flowing through me now.

NO INHERITED DISEASE

There is no inherited tendency to disease or ill health. I am born of Pure Spirit and am free from the belief in material existence.
False ideas cannot be transmitted from one to another, and I am free from all false suggestions.

FOR HEARING

My ears are God's ears; I hear with the ears of Spirit.
I hear the still, small voice of God within me.

FOR EYESIGHT

I can see clearly.
My eyes are the Vision of my Indwelling Spirit. I see with the vision of my Inner Spirit.
I see spiritually, mentally, and physically.

Every idea of the body is now complete and perfect and functions according to the Divine Law.

FREEDOM

I fully and freely forgive everyone. They are free and I am free. I pour out life, love, truth, and beauty to all.

I now declare that I am free from all sense of bondage. I am made perfect and whole through knowledge of the Real Life within me.

I know that there is only One Power, which is God, and I know that this Power now protects me from all harm.

I am not afraid.

I am free from false beliefs.

I walk my own way, immune to all false suggestions.

I live by the One Power, and no thought can enter to disturb me.

My mind is full of peace and poise.

DIVINE GUIDANCE

God is guiding me now; there's right action in my life.

Divine guidance is guiding, guarding, and directing my thoughts and my acts.

Infinite Intelligence governs my thoughts in such a way that I shall always know what to do.

I am identifying myself with success and happiness.

I know that goodness and mercy shall follow me all the days of my life.

I am born of the Spirit,

I am in the Spirit,

I am the Spirit made manifest.

ABOUT THE AUTHOR

Chantha Pak was born in Phnom Penh, Cambodia. Her mother was an entrepreneur, and her father was a doctor.

Chantha's parents passed away when she was five years old, during the Khmer Rouge regime (The Killing Field). Her father was killed by Khmer Rouge, who specifically did not want any intelligent people alive. As a doctor, they took him and other educated people first. This left Chantha an orphan. She was the family's only survivor.

Chantha was adopted by another family who escaped with her on foot to Thailand during the war in 1979. While at the camp in Thailand, they were sponsored by a French family and moved to Dallas, Texas, in 1981. Chantha became a traditional classical dancer at age thirteen, she moved to California in 1984, and she studied the French language for three years.

As was custom at that time, Chantha had an arranged marriage at eighteen years old. She has been married now for over thirty-three years and has two children.

Chantha was a cosmetologist for over thirty-two years and owned her own hair salon. She enjoyed it for so long that it was hard for her to quit! Now she has more time for singing and performing with friends, which she has been doing for over ten years. She still performs at weddings and social events.

Chantha learned the Universal Laws, psychology, and metaphysics from ancient teachers like Florence Scovel Shinn and others. The knowledge of the Power of Mind and how to use it is of the most value to successful living. We all have this latent power within us that we can draw forth and use to improve our lives. Chantha's intention is to help others and to share her knowledge with the world, so anyone in need will also be able to heal themselves.

Connect with Chantha at www.ChanthaPak.com and via email at ChanthaPak@outlook.com.